Tyneside and The Battle of Jutland

31st May 1916

Peter Coppack

Northumbria World War One
Commemoration Project

First Printing: 2016

ISBN 978-1-78280-938-8

Published by:
Northumbria World War One Commemoration Project
C/O Essell
29 Howard Street
North Shields
United Kingdom
NE30 1AR

www.northumbriaworldwarone.co.uk

Preface

This short book is based on the research undertaken for the Northumbria World War One Commemoration Project's exhibition of the same title, produced for the centenary of the battle. With a tight budget, the exhibition was limited in size and format and necessarily prioritised images over text. However, the suggestion that the original draft be turned into an accompanying publication has resulted in this expanded coverage. It makes no pretence at being either a detailed or an academic study but hopes to give the reader an overview of Tyneside's close connections with this very significant but now largely forgotten sea battle.

The author and the project would like to thank the following for their assistance:

Northumbria WW1 Project researchers, especially Linda Green, Valerie Huxtable and Tommy McClemments.

Dot Tose for kindly providing details of her grandfather's and great uncle's service at Jutland.

John Hamilton and the Killingworth World War One Project.

Peter Hoy for sharing his research on South Tyneside casualties.

South Tyneside Library Service, especially Catrin Galt, for picture research and permission to reproduce images. Other images are understood to be in the public domain, but if copyright has been unwittingly infringed, the author apologises and invites the parties concerned to contact the project.

The Royal Navy, especially Lt Matthew Cullen, HMS Echo and Lt Cdr Duncan Young, HMS Calliope. If they get the chance, readers should see The National Museum of the Royal Navy's exhibition: '36 Hours. Jutland 1916: The Battle that Won the War', running in Portsmouth until 2019.

North Tyneside Council for part funding the Northumbria WW1 Project exhibition.

The Heritage Lottery Fund for part funding our exhibition and their ongoing support of the Northumbria WW1 project.

With respect to this book, the author would particularly like to thank Katherine Fidler for initially suggesting its publication, Peter Dixon for his production and design work, Alan Fidler for his encouragement and suggestions, Mike Halsey and Malcolm Dunn for proof reading. Any errors remaining are entirely the author's. If any reader can offer corrections or additional information on any aspect of this book, but particularly local casualties, we would very pleased to hear from them.

Peter Coppack

North Shields,
September 2016

Foreword

One hundred years ago this year, the fleets of the two most powerful maritime nations, met in battle on the seas off the coast of Denmark at the Jutland banks. The battle of Jutland on May 31st, 1916 only last a brief twelve hours but its impact was to change the course of World War One. Only thirty days ago, the last warship sunk due to damage sustained at the battle, was discovered. Untouched, she has held onto her secrets more than 80 metres below.

Other stories have emerged in these last months, many of them due to the efforts of amateur historians – like myself - passionate about preserving the past so that it can be passed to a new generation.

The Northumbria World War One Commemoration Project's *Tyneside and the Battle of Jutland* is such an initiative. The project has added important parts to an evolving jigsaw that is the national commemoration of Jutland.

The connection between Tyneside and Jutland is deep. Some Tyneside-built ships - to name but a few, ships with names like the *Queen Mary, Invincible, Shark* – never returned from the battle. Their stories resonate with the weight of history, loss of life, courage and sacrifice. They touch people and remind us of the maritime tradition of our island nation.

The Armstrong company built many of the ships of Jellicoe's and Beatty's fleets: in all, six battleships, two battlecruisers, three cruisers, sixteen destroyers and even converted the only seaplane carrier to have been in the battle, *HMS Engadine*. Many Tyneside ships as well as others built in the great ports of Great Britain, returned to her harbours and dry-docks to lick their wounds, preparing for renewed battle: *Marlborough*, the only one of Jellicoe's dreadnoughts to be torpedoed, *Lion*, Sir David Beatty's famous flagship, Evan's *Broke*, *Achilles* and, of course, the 935 ton destroyer *Spitfire* which had lost 6 men and suffered a further nine wounded and which herself had nearly met her end in her night ramming of the 20,000 ton German dreadnought, the *SMS Nassau*.

This valuable history speaks of less well-known, but I think equally important episodes: how the community rallied to help wounded survivors and broken families, how families, like the Buchanan family, would see their sons separated on different ships united again on the seas, how the battle took a scythe to many of the old boys from the training ship *Wellesley*, six of whom died on the three battlecruisers lost. The impact on Tyneside, on the families left with the suffering after the loss of loved ones, might not have been on the scale of the manning-ports like Portsmouth or Chatham, but it was certainly very significant.

It is my hope that – following this year's centenary - that the fundamentally crucial task of rescuing and preserving local history and documenting its local impact will not come to an end but will rather continue and encourage others to add their own contributions. Jutland's memory has brought many of us descendants together. In Britain and Germany. New friendships and connections have been made and old ones rebuilt. Like this one. The experience has been both enriching and valuable. And that can only be a good thing.

Nicholas Jellicoe

Jongny, Switzerland
September 2016

Contents

Tyneside And The Battle Of Jutland   1

World War One Warships   2

An Arsenal Economy   5

A Seafaring & Naval Tradition   7

Locally Built Ships At Jutland   8

Anglo-German Naval Rivalry   9

The War At Sea August 1914 - May 1916   13

The Battle   21

The Aftermath Of The Battle on Tyneside   35

The Tyne Rallies To The Navy   39

The Wellesley Training Ship   40

Local Men And Ships Lost   41

Minnows v Leviathans   53

The Adversaries   65

 Jutland – Blame And Scandal   71

Conclusions   75

Aftermath   76

The Fate Of The Dreadnoughts   77

APPENDICES

A Provisional List Of Local Casualties at Jutland   79
HMS Calliope Casualties At Jutland   83

Tyneside And
The Battle Of Jutland
31st May 1916

The Battle of Jutland (or The Skagerakschalcht to the Germans) was a unique event in naval history and the major engagement at sea during the First World War.

It was the only full-scale clash between dreadnought battle-ships. A decade earlier the opposing fleets did not exist - a decade later the development of aircraft and submarines had drastically changed the nature of war at sea.

100 years ago, the eyes of the world turned upon a titanic fight in the North Sea between the Royal Navy's Grand Fleet and the German High Seas Fleet. A new 'Battle of Trafalgar' was anticipated, but instead a confused and unsatisfying sequence of events would create arguments that persist to this day.

With strong traditions of both shipbuilding and seafaring, Tyneside was closely linked to the battle through locally launched warships and the local men who fought and died on them. Tynesiders would be amongst the first to learn of the great battle and the river would provide a haven for ships damaged in the fight: local shipyard workers would be called upon to make herculean efforts to swiftly repair damage so the Royal Navy could be quickly readied for service.

A century later, The Northumbria World War One Commemoration Project explores our region's connections to this key event of the Great War.

World War One Warships

HMS Dreadnought: a battleship

HMS Invincible: a battlecruiser

HMS Warrior: an armoured cruiser

SMS Köln: a light cruiser

HMS Broke: a flotilla leader

HMS Shark: a destroyer

Battleships: the latest designs were the '**dreadnoughts**', a generic term taken from Britain's revolutionary ship of that name. Their armament was focussed on a few heavy guns in four or five large turrets, although secondary batteries of lighter guns were carried. However both Britain and Germany still had older designs of battleships, now called '**pre-dreadoughts**' These tended to carry a wider range of guns of different sizes, with only one or two main gun turrets. They were slower and weaker than the new battleships. The Battle of Tsushima in 1904 (Russo-Japanese War) was fought with pre-dreadoughts.

Battlecruisers: created by Britain's Admiral 'Jackie' Fisher, these battleship sized but lightly armoured vessels carried heavy guns and were designed to quickly reach distant waters to protect British merchant ships or to destroy enemy trade. They could also scout for the battlefleet. They were not intended for a slugging match with heavily armed opposition. Germany built her own battlecruisers in response, but her versions were much better protected.

Battleships and Battlecruisers are often referred to as **Capital Ships**.

Cruisers: a term covering a range of middle-sized warships intended for various roles. **Light cruisers** were designed as scouts for the battlefleets, but could also launch torpedo attacks. **Armoured cruisers** were more heavily armed and protected ships. Some were used for commerce raiding but others could stand up to pre-dreadnought battleships, such as the Tyne-built Japanese armoured cruisers at Tsushima.

Destroyers: small and fast warships originally designed to protect battleships from enemy torpedo boats, hence their original designation as 'torpedo boat destroyers' This was abbreviated to 'destroyer' as the ships also took on the role of attacking with torpedoes. They operated in flotillas led by light cruisers or purpose built large destroyers, known as **Flotilla Leaders**. The crews had very little protection.

The Royal Navy's Grand Fleet at Jutland.

HMS Malaya - one of Britain's latest 'super-dreadnoughts' built on the Tyne by Armstrong's.

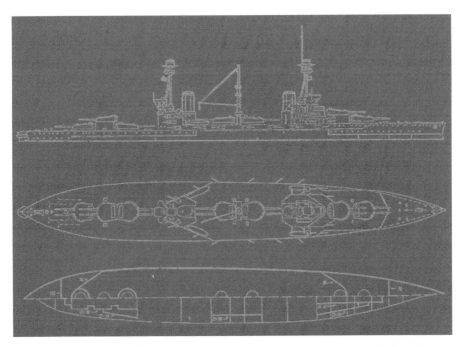

HMS Agincourt - a dreadnought originally built by Armstrong's for the Brazilian Navy but 'taken up' by the Royal Navy.

Death of a Battlecruiser - Jutland incident painted by German war artist Claus Bergen.

An Arsenal Economy

In 1856 Palmer's of Jarrow constructed the Royal Navy's first steam powered armoured vessel: the floating battery HMS Terror In an age of wooden warships the Admiralty had to turn to commercial shipbuilders to obtain the necessary skills to build iron ships. Soon Palmers and the yard's competitors along the river would be building ironclad warships for the navies of the world.

Lord Armstrong's yards at Walker and Elswick, quickly took the lead in constructing modern, fast cruisers armed with guns manufactured in Armstrong's nearby ordnance factory. Heavier armoured cruisers and battleships followed, with Tyne built warships making up a significant component of the Japanese fleet which inflicted the catastrophic defeat on the Russian navy at the battle of Tsushima in 1904 – the greatest modern naval battle before Jutland.

The first decades of the twentieth century saw plenty of naval work for the Tyne's shipbuilders. The fleet's requirements for modern battleships – the dreadnoughts – and the new battlecruisers brought orders to Palmer's and Armstrong's. Warm ties also developed between Tyne yards and the crews of warships entering the Tyne for maintenance and refitting.

With the growing rivalry with Germany, the Tyne was designated a protected port and the river's defences were strengthened with gun batteries at Tynemouth and a submarine mining station at North Shields.

When war came an Admiralty Floating Dock was brought to the Tyne. Jarrow Slake was dredged to permit the dock to be moored in the river, ready to repair warships stationed in this sector of the North Sea. A little way up the coast, Blyth was also provided with gun batteries and the port would become a submarine base in the coming conflict.

The Admiralty Floating Dock on the Tyne.

The Medway Floating Dock AFD4 in 1912.

6

A Seafaring & Naval Tradition

A major port for centuries, the Tyne was home to large numbers of seamen, fishermen and maritime engineers. Some men joined the Royal Navy, who upon leaving the service often continued to sail with the merchant marine with an obligation to return to wartime service as part of the Royal Naval Reserve. Other men were civilians who joined the Royal Naval Volunteer Reserve, some were seamen - particularly fishermen - while others were dockyard workers or even office workers.

Recognising the risk posed by mines highlighted by the recent Russo-Japanese war, the Admiralty offered a subsidy scheme for building fishing trawlers that could quickly be converted to minesweeping duties with volunteer crews, and local fishing firms participated.

HMS Terror - the armoured 'floating battery' built for the Crimean War by Palmer's.

Locally Built Ships At Jutland

Tyne built warships present at Jutland included:

Battleships
HMS Agincourt
HMS Canada
HMS Hercules
HMS Malaya
HMS Monarch
HMS Superb

Battlecruisers
HMS Invincible
HMS Queen Mary

Cruisers
HMS Birmingham
HMS Champion
HMS Comus

Destroyers
HMS Badger
HMS Christopher
HMS Contest
HMS Marksman
HMS Mary Rose
HMS Martial
HMS Menace
HMS Nessus
HMS Nestor
HMS Noble
HMS Nonsuch
HMS Shark
HMS Sparrowhawk
HMS Spitfire
HMS Termagent
HMS Turbulent

Seaplane Carriers
HMS Engadine, which briefly played a role in locating the German fleet at Jutland, was converted from a passenger ferry at Palmer's.

HMS Queen Mary leaving the Tyne, 1913. (South Tyneside Libraries)

Anglo - German Naval Rivalry

From the mid-eighteenth century, Britain's navy had dominated the oceans allowing the nation to build a global trading network and the world's largest colonial empire. Despite tensions with her colonial rivals (primarily France and Russia) Britain's position was not challenged during the ninenteenth century. However from the 1890s this changed when the new German Kaiser Wilhelm II - Queen Victoria's doting grandson – began to demand Germany too should have "its place in the sun" of empire, and supported Admiral Tirpitz's plan to turn the small German Navy into a major naval force able to challenge the Royal Navy's pre-eminence.

In 1906 the Royal Navy made the drastic decision to introduce a new design of battleship, HMS Dreadnought, far more powerful than any other warship - but at the same time making the rest of Britain's battle fleet obsolete. Germany took the opportunity to build its own dreadnoughts and create a new fleet from scratch. The stage was set for a naval arms race throughout the decade preceding the outbreak of the Great War.

Admiral John Arbuthnot Fisher; driving force behind the Royal Navy's Dreadnought programme.

Admiral Alfred von Turpitz; architect of Germany's new fleet.

The battlecruiser SMS Seydlitz with a Zeppelin overhead - symbols of
German technical progress.

The First and Second Battleship Squadrons of the German High Seas
Fleet.

Without the Royal Navy's legacy of a large pre-existing fleet of battleships (some fairly new but already outclassed), the German Navy could focus on building up a force of modern ships whose design emphasised the defensive strength needed to take on a numerically superior opponent.

Yet despite the Kaiser's enthusiastic support, a battlefleet would always be a luxury for a continental power and Germany's army took priority in funding. The new German capital ships were designed for relatively limited operations of no more than a week in the North Sea. Their crews spent their time in barracks when not at sea and the ships' complements were only at full strength when reservists joined them for annual training cruises. Despite these limitations, the German High Seas Fleet was forged into a potent weapon.

In contrast the Royal Navy possessed centuries of naval tradition, epitomised by Lord Nelson and the Battle of Trafalgar. This encouraged daring and aggression in battle, although it may have also given rise to complacency and over confidence. The Royal Navy was the pride of Britain and her Empire and could command the lion's share of the defence budget.

British warship design stressed speed and firepower at the expense of armour - especially for the new battlecruisers which joined the dreadnoughts. Armour was also sacrificed up to a point to provide more habitable on-board accommodation for ships' crews who might have to fight anywhere in the world - although the Grand Fleet began to be concentrated at Scapa Flow in response to the German threat. Its sailors lived and trained on their ships, and although reservists did serve on board, they were there to supplement a highly professional permanent crew.

HMS Invincible anchored at Spithead - the battlecruisers were a radical concept of Admiral 'Jackie' Fisher.

The Kaiser in Naval uniform (left) discusses his fleet with its architect Admiral Turpitz (centre).

The War At Sea
August 1914 - May 1916

The Naval Blockade of Germany

From the first weeks of the war the Royal Navy initiated its tradi-
tional strategy against a hostile continental power – the blockade
of the enemy's ports. These duties, and the complementary work
of protecting British merchant shipping from German raiders and
the U-boat counter-blockade, were the ongoing routine of the war
at sea. Largely unseen by the press and public, only occasionally
did naval actions make the headlines. The desire to permanently
break this blockade was the underlying motivation for the
German operation at Jutland.

The Battle of Heligoland

On 28th August 1914, a British sweep by destroyers across the
North Sea tested the defences of the German fortress island of
Heligoland. After initial success against German destroyers, the
attacking force was threatened by heavier German ships, only to
be saved by the arrival of British cruisers. These in turn risked
destruction by German battlecruisers until the sudden appear-
ance of Vice Admiral Beatty's battlecruiser force. The British with-
drew without loss claiming victory after sinking three light cruisers. However the action revealed a disconcerting lack of co-ordination between the separate British squadrons. German losses
shook the Kaiser's confidence and he insisted that his navy avoid
future high risk operations. As a consequence the High Seas Fleet
only rarely ventured out – much to the frustration of the British.

The sinking of German torpedo boat V187 at Heligoland, 1914.

The German light cruiser Magdeburg at Coronel, Chile.

The Sinking of HMSs Hogue, Cressy & Aboukir

On the morning of 22nd September 1914, three British cruisers were sunk by German submarine U-9 in quick succession with great loss of life. At first it was assumed that mines were to blame (these had been the main threat to Japanese battleships a decade earlier). The attack indicated the threat submarines now posed and highlighted the lack of underwater protection in many warship designs.

The Battle of Coronel

Admiral Graf Maximilian von Spee led Germany's East Asiatic Squadron of five cruisers on an epic voyage raiding allied shipping across the Pacific, chased by the embarassed British and Japanese navies. At Coronel off the coast of Chile, he encountered and completely destroyed a Royal Navy force consisting of two armoured and one light cruiser. This humiliating defeat prompted the British Admiralty to quickly despatch a strong force of modern warships.

The Battle of the Falklands

Admiral von Spee's force was finally overwhelmed and sunk by the British battlecruisers Invincible and Inflexible while attempting an attack on Port Stanley on 8th December 1914. The victory reaffirmed Britain's confidence in her navy and seemed to vindicate Fisher's battlecruiser concept. The Royal Navy was able to hunt down and destroy Germany's other surface raiders, forcing her to rely on U-boats to attack Britain's trade routes.

British battlecruisers sink the light cruiser Coln at the Battle of Heligoland - a role they were designed for.

Hans Bohrdt's painting 'The Last Man' - a German propaganda postcard
following the Falklands action.

The Bombardment of Hartlepool, Whitby and Scarborough

In the early hours of 16th December 1914, the German Navy's battlecruisers bombarded Hartlepool, Whitby and Scarborough. The attacks caused serious damage and many civilian casualties. The Germans achieved a propaganda coup – and a successful diversion while their cruisers laid mines off the English coast. However they did not manage to lure any part of the Grand Fleet into an advantageous battle as hoped.

The raids created anxiety in parts of Britain near the sea, but fuelled the call for volunteers to fight against Germany's "frightfulness".

The Battle of The Dogger Bank

26th January 1915 - another German operation aimed at drawing part of the Royal Navy into battle. The ploy worked when Admiral Beatty took his battlecruisers into action against their German opposite numbers. Although the loss of the German heavy cruiser Blücher allowed the British to claim victory, a direct hit to a gun turret on Beatty's flagship HMS Lion came close to destroying the ship. Beatty's force also displayed poor signalling and co-ordination between the battlecruisers and the battleship squadron supporting him. The damaged Lion and other ships came to the Tyne for repair after this action.

The German battlecruiser raid on Hartlepool resulted in civilian deaths and a strong desire for vengeance by the Royal Navy.

The loss of the Lusitania is credited with helping to bring the USA into the war on the side of the Allies.

The Sinking of The Lusitania

The Cunard liner RMS Lusitania was sunk in sight of the Irish
coast on 7th May 1915 with great loss of civilian life, including
many neutral Americans. Germany commemorated the event
with a medal, but the sinking caused outrage on both sides of the
Atlantic and eventually helped bring the United States into the
war on the side of the allies in 1917. The death toll added to
anti-German sentiment in Britain and a popular desire for vengeance against the German navy.

The U-boat Campaign

Hundreds of merchant vessels would be sunk by German U-boats
and mines during the war, even before the commencement of
unrestricted submarine warfare in 1917. Many Tynesiders died in
these attacks and others risked – and often lost – their lives
serving on board fishing trawlers and other vessels pressed into
naval service as minesweepers or anti-submarine patrol boats.

A German submarine raider.

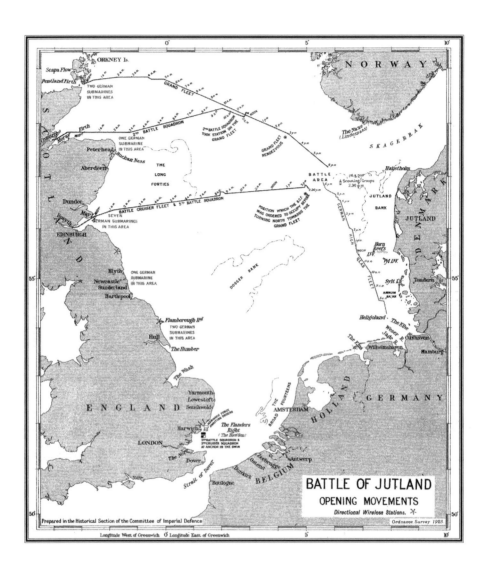

BATTLE OF JUTLAND
OPENING MOVEMENTS
Directional Wireless Stations.

The Battle

*"The brunt of the fighting fell on the British battlecruiser
fleet supported by four battleships, some light cruisers and
a destroyer squadron. Soon after our main forces appeared
on the scene the German fleet broke off the engagement and
made a hurried return to their base, though not before
receiving a severe mauling from our battleships."*
Admiral Jellicoe

"A most enjoyable little scrap" Captain JW Farqhuar to his
father, Admiral Sir Arthur Farqhuar

The battle plans of the British Grand Fleet under Admiral Jellicoe
and the German High Seas Fleet under Admiral Scheer in many
ways mirrored each other. The Germans continued their strategy
of trying to draw out and trap part of the Royal Navy in a battle
where they had local superiority, prior to a full scale battle with a
reduced Grand Fleet that the Germans could hope to win. The
British aim was to track down the German High Seas Fleet at sea
and manouvre between the German ships and their home port,
trapping the Germans into fighting an all out battle that the Royal
Navy was confident it would win.

The initial German plan was to bombard Sunderland to draw out
Admiral Beatty's battlecruisers and battleships from the Firth of
Forth. U-boats were to be stationed off the coast to ambush the
British forces before they reached the German fleet. Adverse
weather led to the abandonment of the Sunderland attack, but the
German fleet still went out and the U-boats were deployed –
although they failed to intercept any British ships.

Vice Admiral David Beatty - impetuous commander of Britain's battlecruisers.

Admiral Sir John Jellicoe commander of the Grand Fleet - 'the only man on either side who could have lost the war in an afternoon'.

Vice Admiral Franz Ritter von Hipper - commander of the superb German battlecruiser force.

Admiral Reinhard von Scheer - commander of Germany's High Seas Fleet.

22

The British were able to read German naval codes and had picked up the radio signals indicating the Germans were heading to sea. Admiral Jellicoe's Grand Fleet departed Scapa Flow and Beatty's force set sail from the Forth, to rendezvous in the North Sea and commence a sweep to find the Germans and at last bring them to battle.

"We were thinking that we would still be able to get back again for our leave this week and the sole topic of conversation was that and what we were going to do on our holiday". Sailor on HMS Lion

During the morning of 31st May, in poor weather and limited visibility, both fleets sent out light cruisers to try to locate the enemy. Around 2pm British and German scouts spotted a neutral Danish steamer, the Naesborg, and went to investigate. As they closed on the steamer the opposing warships sighted each other and signalled their respective fleets.

Beatty's force was sailing some 15 miles ahead of the main British force. When he learned that the Germans had been located he steamed at high speed in their direction, leaving his slower but more powerful battleships behind without briefing their commander Admiral Evan-Thomas, who was left to follow as quickly as he could. The seaplane carrier HMS Engadine launched an aircraft to help with the search, but after spotting Admiral Hipper's battlecruisers at 3.29pm the pilot was ordered to land and no more flights were made. Meanwhile the Danish steamer and at least two other neutral craft had to get clear of the battle as best they could.

"During the fight the cannonading was so violent, that the crew of the Naesborg could not stand erect on deck" The Illustrated Chronicle 3rd June 1916

Soon the two battlecruiser fleets came within range and firing commenced, while the Germans began to lead the British towards

The High Seas Fleet flagship at Jutland, SMS Friedrich Der Grosse.

Britain's Grand Fleet deploys at Jutland.

their battle fleet. German gunnery was accurate and directed at all the British ships. For some reason the British failed to target one German ship which fired on them unmolested for quarter of an hour. British gunnery was not very accurate and when hits were made some of the shells disintegrated instead of penetrating German armour (these duds were christened "Yankees" since they were "too proud to fight"). At about 4pm, after only a few salvoes HMS Indefatigable was hit by a single shell and simply exploded, going down with most of her thousand strong crew. Beatty's flagship, HMS Lion, was struck in the turret previously hit at Dogger Bank, and admiral and ship were only saved by the turret crew's self-sacrifice in flooding their magazine. The 'Run to the South' towards the enemy continued, with HMS Queen Mary hit and exploding at 4.26pm, prompting Beatty to comment,

"There seems to be something wrong with our bloody ships today."

While Beatty's force was some miles ahead of Jellicoe, the battleships of the German High Seas Fleet closed on Beatty's ships and they soon faced the full force of the German fleet. A jubilant Scheer had the British battlecruiser force and the five supporting battleships massively outnumbered.

Realising the danger, Beatty ordered his battle cruiser squadrons to turn back towards the Grand Fleet, but the signal to Evan Thomas' battleships was delayed and they almost ran into the High Seas Fleet. The first four turned before the Germans had their range, but the last ship, the Armstrong built HMS Malaya, turned under concentrated enemy fire, suffering several hits before escaping. The Germans pursued the retreating British ships thinking victory was close.

The light cruiser HMS Galatea was the first ship to spot the Germans.

"We drew the enemy into the jaws of our fleet. I have no regret except for the lives of gallant pals who have gone, but who died gloriously. It would have done your heart good to have seen how gallantly Hood brought his squadron into action. Would to God he had been more successful in the result." Admiral Beatty

Jellicoe was closing on the Germans but did not know their exact position or heading, with only vague information coming from Beatty. Without a clearer picture Jellicoe did not know how best to deploy his battle line, but decided to draw out his ships in a line to the north. He sent Admiral Hood's force of 3 battlecruisers to reinforce Beatty who was rapidly approaching, in what became known as the "Run to the North".

Beatty reached the British fleet and crossed in front of it, while Evan-Thomas took his battleships to join the Grand Fleet's battle line. Hipper's pursuing squadron came upon Hood's battlecruisers and their supporting flotillas. During this sharp exchange of fire, 16 year old Boy 1st Class Jack Cornwell earned his posthumous VC on HMS Chester. A German salvo hit Hood's flagship HMS Invincible, which exploded as the two other battleships had earlier. However the German battlecruisers had little time to celebrate as they came under fire from the Grand Fleet and were forced to turn away.

"Gefechtskehrtwendung nach steurbord!" (**Battle turn to starboard!**) Admiral Scheer to High Seas Fleet

Jellicoe's deployment proved correct for he found that he was in a position to "cross the T" of the German line as they approached, allowing the majority of his ships to fire on the Germans, who could not return fire because of the ships in the line ahead of them. The British battleships threw out rapid and accurate salvoes. Scheer realised he could not survive such an encounter and ordered his battleships to perform a rehearsed battle turn away from the British, while his destroyers and light cruisers fired waves of torpedoes towards the approaching enemy, and laid down a smoke screen to hide their capital ships as they sped away into the mist.

Inside a battleship's main turret during the battle - painting by Imperial German Navy artist Claus Bergen.

His Majesty's Ship Derfflinger - one of the Kaiser's battlecruisers, possibly the best capital ships of their day.

The seaplane carrier HMS Engadine launched a spotting plane early in the battle but would play no further part. Jutland would be the last major naval battle in which aircraft did not play a decisive role.

"If, for instance, the enemy Battle Fleet were to turn away from an advancing fleet, I should assume that the intention was to lead us over mines and submarines, and should decline to be so drawn. I desire particularly to draw the attention of their Lordships to this point since it may be deemed a refusal of battle, and indeed might possibly result in failure to bring an enemy to action as soon as is expected and hoped. Such a result would be absolutely repugnant to the feelings of all British naval officers and men, but with new and untried methods of warfare new tactics must be devised to meet them."
Admiral Jellicoe to the Admiralty, October 1914.

Jellicoe turned away through fear of losing capital ships to torpedoes. He had agreed this policy with the Admiralty in the first months of the war. It was later said that never before had one man on either side been in a position to lose the war in an afternoon – if the Royal Navy had lost several battleships to torpedoes the Germans may have been in a position to fulfil their ambition of decisively defeating the Royal Navy. In contrast Beatty had always advocated closing with the enemy, regardless of British losses, and he was impatient to chase after the Germans:

"Urgent. Submit van of battleships follows battlecruisers. We can then cut off the whole enemy's battlefleet".
Admiral Beatty to Admiral Jellicoe

Only after the torpedo threat had passed, did Jellicoe permit the British pursuit to be renewed, and the Grand Fleet again began closing the distance with the High Seas Fleet.

"Schlachtkreuzer ran an den Feind, voll einsetzen!" (**"Battlecruisers at the enemy, give it everything!"**)
Admiral Scheer to Vice Admiral Hipper

At 7.13pm Admiral Scheer ordered his battlecruisers to make a further attack against the British fleet in a "death ride" to cover

The German pre-dreadnought Pommern was the only battleship sunk during the battle.

the withdrawal of his High Seas Fleet. The battlecruisers suffered a severe beating, with the flagship Lützow fatally hit, the Seydlitz only just managed to remain afloat and the Derfflinger suffered massive damage. However the resilience of the German ships was enormous and enabled the surviving vessels to get clear of the British and make their way home independently of Scheer.

The courses of the two battle fleets began to resemble a 'V', the British sailing South and the Germans South East, both closing on the other, but unaware of the other's presence in the failing light. The German Official History declared that it was one of the most curious incidents in naval history that the two fleets did not come together at the 'V's" point:

"Tiny factors, and no human plan, caused Jellicoe to arrive at the bottom of the V and pass through the junction point short minutes before the German ships arrived. The 'V' became an 'X' – the courses of the fleets reversed, neither side was conscious of what was happening – and from then onward they began to draw apart." Der Krieg In Der Nordsee

As night fell and in poor visibility, the two fleets separated – the Germans looking for a safe route home, the British recovering their order and commencing a fresh search for the enemy, hoping to catch them the next morning before they reached port. Unaware of each other's position, the two battle fleets remained at action stations, while skirmishes between light forces continued.

"...it was literally awful – far worse and utterly different to anything I've been through in daylight" Commander M L Goldsmith

Around 2am a squadron of British destroyers and accompanying cruisers to the rear of the Grand Fleet stumbled into the middle of the enemy battle line. They commenced a series of desperately brave but unco-ordinated attacks on the German capital ships. The Royal Navy had little training in night actions but the Germans had been prepared for this. The old pre-dreadnought Pommern was was sunk and several escorting cruisers and destroyers set ablaze, but the British ships were shot to pieces by the German battleships. None of them signalled to the Grand Fleet that they had found the Germans and while the gunfire could be heard, Jellicoe was not informed of its origin. He was also not told that the Admiralty had picked up Scheer's wireless request for a zeppelin to reconnoitre the Horn Reef – a clear indication of the German route home.

Thus Scheer and his fleet escaped, although many of his ships were badly damaged and required months to repair. Once it was clear that the enemy had returned to base, the Royal Navy set sail for its home ports, passing over the scene of the battle and seeing hundreds of dead bodies floating in the sea, as well as scores of fish killed by the concussion of shells. Later some of the warships encountered the Tyne fishing fleet, the first civilians to hear news of the battle. That evening battered ships began to arrive at North Shields.

A German dreadnought photographed from a Zeppelin - at Jutland the airships failed to give Scheer advance warning of the Grand Fleet's movements.

"...the superior gunnery and tactics of the British Fleet enabled them to withstand the shock of the thunderous battle marvelously well" The Illustrated Chronicle 3rd June 1916

"We are ready for the next time; please God it will come soon. The British fleet is alive, and has a very big kick in him!"
Admiral Beatty

"The events of the last few days have been, to some of us, more than we could bear. Thousands have been killed – men I have known all my life...It is very difficult for naval officers to speak in the calm way they would like".
Admiral Sir Edward Mieux, 6th June 1916

"The German fleet has assaulted its jailor, but is still in gaol"
US Newspaper

"...even the most successful outcome of a fleet action in this war will not force England to make peace."
Admiral Scheer, 4th July 1916

King George V addresses the Grand Fleet after the battle.

"I don't think it was nearly such a bad show for us as the losses show"
Commander T S Fox Pitt, HMS Inflexible, writing to his brother
in the army, June 1916

Summary of Losses at Jutland

	British	German
Battleships	0	1
Battlecruiser	3	1
Armoured Cruisers	3	0
Light Cruisers	0	4
Destroyers	8	5
Total vessels sunk	14	11
Crew killed	6097	2551
Crew wounded	510	517
Taken as POW	177	0
Total Crew Casualties	6784	3058
Percentage of Total Ships Companies Engaged	8.84%	6.79%

After the battle, allowing for capital ships damaged and in dry
dock, the Royal Navy retained a 9:7 advantage over the German
fleet.

The Aftermath Of Battle On Tyneside

As Scapa Flow had no facilities to undertake the heavy repair work, the battlecruisers and other ships that had seen the hottest action during the battle headed for the Firth of Forth and the Tyne where shipyards were made ready to receive them.

Many of these yards were already filled with ships undergoing refits or repairs and they had to be quickly cleared. Smith's Dock were notified at 9.15pm on 31st May that they needed to carry out the emergency undocking of the cruiser HMS Achilles by 4.15am the following morning. The yard called in its workforce and got the job done so quickly that the Tyne's Captain Superintendent praised their efforts in writing:

"It is very satisfactory to feel how thoroughly I can rely upon the cooperation of your firm in such emergencies, which are or may be of national importance, and, in my opinion, it reflects the greatest credit upon the organisation, and shows how good a touch there must be between the management and the employees that the men could be collected at short notice and so successfully carry out the work required."

Admiral Beatty's flagship, HMS Lion, with a knocked out gun turret and other damage, entered the Tyne – just as she had after Dogger Bank. It was reported that when the flooded magazine beneath the turret was opened, the bodies of the drowned crewmen still grasped the watertight doors they had closed to save the ship.

HMS Broke, A destroyer flotilla leader entered the river missing most of her bow – she had been rammed by a British cruiser in

IN MEMORY OF JUTLAND HEROES

ADMIRAL WILLIAM F. SLAYTER (marked with an arrow) attended the service held at sea off the Tyne in memory of the men who fell in the battle of Jutland. Below are blue-jackets firing three volleys over the stern of the vessel.

The Tyne witnessed the funeral of Stoker Monk in North Shields, and this service at sea off the mouth of the Tyne for the Navy's dead.

the confused night battle against the German battleships. She went straight into a Palmer's dry dock. Another destroyer arrived with a funnel and much of her superstructure smashed in. HMS Marlborough arrived at the Tyne after her torpedoing and was taken into the Admiralty Floating Dock in Jarrow Slake to be repaired. It was found that she had a lucky escape. The bodies of her two dead crewmen were brought ashore in North Shields.

The remains of one man were sent by rail to Manchester, but the other, Stoker 2nd Class Edgar George Monk was to be buried in Preston Cemetery, North Shields. While arrangements were made his body lay in a temporary chapel fitted out for the purpose in the Tynemouth Victoria Jubilee Infirmary.

On 9th of June the whole town turned out for his full naval and military funeral, with a firing party of 28 sailors, a combined band of the Duke of Wellington's Regiment and the Royal Marines. The coffin was draped with the Union Jack and a wreath and drawn on a gun carriage by 2 horses, escorted by the Tyne Royal Garrison Artillery. Large numbers of floral tributes were carried by files of naval ratings. The senior naval officer present *"expressed his thanks to the mayor for the kind and sympathetic consideration extended to the Naval men in the Tyne by the civil population."*

The Shields Daily News declared it to be: *"one of the most impressive spectacles ever witnessed in North Shields."*

The badly damaged destroyer HMS Spitfire enters the Tyne.

Destroyer Leader HMS Broke in dry dock at Palmer's following the battle.

The Tyne Rallies To The Navy

Injured seamen were placed in hospitals around the area and local people rallied to support them. Local car owners brought their cars to act as ambulances and an appeal was made for walking sticks, books and games for the sailors in local hospitals. The press reported that, although the Admiralty paid for the necessaries of life, they needed more and an appeal was started by Messrs Randall and Forsyth of the Tynemouth Grocers' Association. Christ Church Girls' School, North Shields, presented them with £2. 10s collected from the teachers and scholars for *"our dear, brave men"*. Wallsend Council passed a resolution recording their *"admiration for the magnificent courage and devotion and skill displayed by the officers and men of His Majesty's Navy."*

A concert was organised for the crews of the ships in the Albion Assembly Rooms, North Shields, on the 14th June. The Shield's Daily News reported: another "first class concert" was arranged ten days later for the naval patients in Leitch Ward of the Jubilee Infirmary. Madame Burns sang solos, including *"When You Come Home"* at the express wish of one of the men; while Miss Evelyn Waggott's classical dances proved,*"a prime favourite with the sailors...she had to give her balloon dance three times"*.

In the shipyards, management and workers settled past differences to get the ships ready for service as quickly as possible. The local boilermakers' and engineers' union committee recommended that its members should forego their week of annual holiday, instead taking leave in tranches of a quarter of the workers at a time. On the Floating Dock arrangements were made for the workers to sleep and eat on board so 24 hour working could be maintained.

The men fighting in France were too far away for the population to offer direct support, but the heroes of Jutland were close at hand and Tyneside appears to have responded with an outpouring of patriotic feeling and support for the fleet.

The Wellesley Training Ship

Wellesley boys on parade.

The loss of the old sailing ship.

The Wellesley School was originally a former wooden man o' war that was anchored at North Shields and used as a school for boys from across England who were deemed at risk of falling into bad company and criminality. Sadly the old warship was destroyed by fire a few months before the outbreak of the Great War, and the school was relocated first to Tynemouth, then to Blyth. Many of the boys who had trained on board went on to serve in the Royal Navy during the war. Tragically, a number would die in the conflict and several were lost at Jutland. The sacrifice of the school's old boys prompted one local paper to exclaim, *"what the ship has done for the nation"*!

Old boys lost include:

HMS Indefatigable - E Tait: Newcastle,
                    J Bennett: Tyneside
                    J Michaux: Oxford
HMS Queen Mary – W Atkinson: Tynemouth,
                    J Kelly: Dewsbury
HMS Invincible –   A Hold: Middlesbrough

Local Men And Ships Lost

HMS Indefatigable 18,800 tons – crew 853

HMS Indefatigable was a battlecruiser built at Devonport and launched in 1911. She was one of the lead ships of Beatty's force as they attacked Hipper's battlecruisers at the start of the battle. She was engaged by the SMS Von der Tann and exploded only 19 minutes after HMS Galatea had first spotted the German force. Indefatigable was the first capital ship lost in the battle.

Able Seaman Robert Hunter Weatherstone RNVR, born 1st February 1895 in North Shields,was a manager at W S Hedley grocers before the war. He joined the Royal Naval Division in August 1915, later transferring to the Indefatigable. A notice of his death was published in the Shields Daily News: *'Lost through the foundering of HMS Indefatigable...dearly beloved sweetheart of Alice Downey. The hand I clasped when saying good-bye lies now in death's cold chill'.*

John Wigan Bennett was born in 1897 and attended the Wellesley school 1909 -13 until he joined the Royal Navy.

Able Seaman Ernest Houghland, born 11th December 1896 in Sheffield, was one of the Wellesley old boys lost on the battlecruiser.

Able Seaman James Michaux was born in Cape Town South Africa, in 1897, the adopted son of Rachel J Walker of Oxford, he was yet another Wellesley boy who died.

Signalman Richard Henry Lock from South Tyneside.

HMS Indefatigable - the first British casualty at Jutland.

HMS Queen Mary passing down the Tyne after completion in 1913.

HMS Queen Mary 29,700 tons - crew 1,061

Described as "Jarrow's own ship" in the local press, HMS Queen Mary was a battlecruiser built by Palmer's and launched in 1913. She was the second battlecruiser to explode and split in half at 4.26pm.

Incredibly a handful of men did survive, although the crew remained at their posts to the end. One survivor was gunnery Petty Officer Ernest Francis, who recorded his experiences inside one of the ship's main gun turrets in the moments after the "big smash":

"Everything in the ship went as quiet as a church, the floor of the turret was bulged up and the guns were absolutely useless. I must mention here that there was not a sign of excitement...I went back to the Cabinet [Lt Ewart's station, the turret commander] and said, "What do you think has happened, Sir?" He said, "God knows!" "Well Sir," I said, "It's no use keeping them all down here. Why not send them up on the 4" guns, and give them a chance to fight it out? As soon as the Germans find we are out of action they will concentrate on us and we shall all be going sky high." He said, "Yes, good idea, just see if the 4" guns aft are still standing."

Francis looked out of the hole in the turret roof and saw that the aft 4" guns had been completely destroyed and that the ship was now beginning to list alarmingly. He reported what he had observed to Lt Ewart.

He said, "Francis, we can do no more than give them a chance, clear the turret". "Clear the turret," I said, and out they went. PO Stevens was the last I saw coming up from the working chamber, and I asked him whether he had passed the order to the Magazine and Shell Room, and he told me it was no use as the water was right up to the trunk leading to the shell room, so the bottom of the ship must have been torn out of her. Then I said, "Why didn't you come up?" He simply said, "there was no order to leave the turret."

Warrant Engineer F. E. White, of North
Shields, lost with the Queen Mary.

JAMES F. GRAHAM,
of North Shields.
(Lost with the Queen Mary.)

Local men lost with the Queen Mary.

German postcard of the explosion which ripped HMS Queen Mary apart.
HMS Lion is to the left, straddled by giant shell splashes.

Francis left the turret with Lt Ewart following closely behind, only to find that the officer had turned back. He would not see Ewart again,

"I believe he went back because he thought someone was inside. I cannot say enough for Lt Ewart, nothing I can say would do him justice. He came out of the turret cabinet twice and yelled out something to encourage the gun crew, and yelled out to me, "All right, Francis". He was grand, and I would like to publish this account to the World. It makes me feel sore hearted when I think of Lt Ewart and the fine crowd who were with me in the turret."

Francis had great difficulty climbing down the ladder at the back of the turret because of the Queen Mary's increasing list. Trying to get up the deck to the side of the ship was impossible without the help of two other members of the turret crew. Once he reached the ship's side he found a large group of the crew who were reluctant to leave the ship:

"I called out to them, "Come on you chaps, who's coming for a swim?" Someone answered, "She'll float for a long time yet", but something, I don't pretend to know what it was, seemed to be urging me to get away, so I clambered over the slimy bilge keel and fell off into the water, followed I should think by about five more men. I struck away from the ship as hard as I could and must have covered nearly fifty yards when there was a big smash, and stopping and looking round, the air seemed to be full of fragments and flying pieces. I dipped under to avoid being struck, and stayed under for as long as I could, and then came to the top again, and coming behind me I heard a rush of water, which looked very like surf breaking on a beach and I realised it was the suction or backwash from the ship which had just gone. I hardly had time to fill my lungs with air when it was on me. I felt it was no use struggling against it, so I let myself go for a moment or two, then struck out, but felt it was a losing game and remarked to myself, "What's the use of you struggling, you're done", and I actually ceased any efforts to reach the top, when a small voice seemed to say "Dig out".

Francis was eventually rescued by HMS Petard and taken to her sick bay Temporarily blinded by oil covering the water, he was unaware of a German shell ripping through the destroyer and killing the doctor who was tending to his eyes. He was eventually brought back to Rosyth at midnight on the 1st June. Another eyewitness on the cruiser HMS Dublin witnessed Queen Mary's final seconds:

"In every detail we could see officers and signalmen with others as the ship, already doing 20 knots with the fore section blown forward, carving a higher bow wave than before only listing slightly to port, then skidding round starboard towards Dublin...We actually pointed our helm to avoid her hitting us but it proved unnecessary; with increasing list she dived, her fore turret guns at full elevation hot with firing, giving off a loud hissing as they met the water. It was terrible to see those poor souls so near yet so far and being unable to help"

The Queen Mary's destruction was also watched by the crew of her German opponent:

"a livid red flame shot up from her forepart; then came an explosion amidships. Immediately afterwards she blew up with a terrific explosion, the masts collapsing inwards and the smoke hiding everything."

Only 18 of her 1, 289 crew were saved. Nearly a third of the Jutland casualties from Tyneside identified by the Northumbria World War One Project served on the Queen Mary, suggesting a strong local affinity with this particular ship.

Earnest Frederick White, of Hylton Street, North Shields had survived the sinking of HMS Hogue 1914. Before the war he was employed by Smiths Dock Co Ltd in the pontoons department. He joined the Royal Naval Reserve at the start of the war and became an Engine Room Artificer on HMS Queen Mary, *"a young man of fine physique and attractive character, he had a great many friends in North Shields".*

Edward Tait of Heaton, Newcastle, was a Wellesley boy who joined the Royal Navy, and served as an Able Seaman on Queen Mary.

George Stanley Kewney was born in Tynemouth in 1874. He attended Pembroke College, Cambridge and became a Cricket Blue, before joining the Church of England to become the curate at Corbridge. There he made a name for the Corbridge Cricket Club in West Tynedale. He married Lydia Cousins Stephens, of Ravenstone, in Hexham in 1900 and the young couple moved to Devon when he became a Royal Navy Chaplain. Sadly Lydia died but he remarried Catherine Margaret Bain-Currie.Their daughter Margaret was born in 1914. Kewney was a chaplain on several ships including HMS Dreadnought, before joining the Queen Mary and was Instructor to the future King George VI when a midshipman in the Royal Navy.

James Francis Graham of North Shields was a carpenter in the Tyne Commissioners Yard at Howdon, before serving in the Royal Naval Volunteer Reserve as an Able Seaman on Queen Mary, "deeply mourned" by his wife Margaret (nee Hudson)

Charles Waugh, Stoker 1st Class (born 1893) was a coal miner from West Moor, Forest Hall.

George Dodd, Leading Stoker (born 1890) originally came from Romsey, Hampshire and was the son of a gamekeeper, but after his father's death his mother remarried a miner from the north. He was also a miner from West Moor, as was a third:

James Robson Swinney, Stoker, born 1897 in Alnwick, his mother's home town.

Invincible caught on camera a split second before she was ripped apart.
Her midship turrets are already an exploding fireball. Crown Copyright

P. CALLENDER

Engine Room Artificer Peter
Callender, lost with the ship.

HMS Invincible - the first battlecruiser.

HMS Invincible 17,250 tons – crew 1,031

HMS Invincible was the Royal Navy's first battlecruiser, launched at Armstrong's Elswick shipyard in 1908. Invincible played a key role in Admiral Sturdee's task force at the Falklands in 1914, and thereafter the ship's Stoker's Band named themselves, "Sturdee's Rascals".

During the battle she was Admiral Hood's flagship for the 3rd Battlecruiser Squadron, attached to Jellicoe's main force. This squadron was sent to support Beatty after he turned towards the Grand Fleet with the Germans in pursuit. Lion had signalled the enemy's position to Black Prince, but Lion made a dead reckoning error which resulted in Invincible's squadron coming closer to the German battlecruisers than intended. Invincible had just completed several weeks gunnery practice at Scapa Flow, so her salvoes against the Germans were accurate. Hood signalled,

"Your fire is very good! Keep it up as quickly as you can! Every shot is telling."

However a German shell penetrated Invincible and she exploded like the Indefatigable and Queen Mary. Initially her centre turrets exploded, but a split second later a jet of flame shot up under her forward turret as the internal shell magazines detonated. This instant was captured on camera: although the ship appears largely intact in the photograph, her interior was already a raging inferno. A second later the ship split in two. The two pieces of the hull remained afloat for nearly 24 hours before they sank.

HMS Marlborough 25,000 tons – crew 1,022

A battleship in Jellicoe's Grand Fleet, she was torpedoed at 6.57pm and hit in the engine room.

It now seems likely that this was the last shot of the sinking Wiesbaden, which had been scouting ahead of the High Seas Fleet when British battlecruisers quickly reduced her to a flaming wreck; however her crew fought on until the end. The torpedo explosion killed two stokers and damaged boilers and machinery, but it did not prevent Marlborough from continuing in the action.

After turning away from the German torpedo attack covering their High Seas Fleet's battle turn, Jellicoe ordered the Royal Navy's battleships to renew their pursuit at 8.55pm. This was premature as further German torpedoes came towards the Grand Fleet. Again, HMS Marlborough was at risk, evading the trails of two torpedoes by turns to port and starboard. However a third torpedo tracked directly under the ship, only to fail to explode – a bit of good luck given her already compromised condition.

Her luck did not extend to getting revenge on the enemy. At 12.45am Marlborough sighted the heavily damaged Seydlitz in the darkness, and her gunnery officer brought her main armament to bear on the distant target and sought his captain's permission to fire. This was refused for fear of hitting a British ship. The officer concerned, Lt Commander Guy Royle later commented,

"...of course what I ought to have done was to have opened fire and blown the ship out of the water and then said "sorry"!"

The following day Marlborough made for the Tyne for repairs and was taken into the Admiralty Floating Dock (AFD4) in Jarrow Slake. Smith's Dock Company later noted that she had a lucky escape as the damage was more serious than initially thought.

HMS Marlborough

HMS Marlborough in action at Jutland

Damage to HMS Malaya

SMS Wiesbaden

SMS Wiesbaden and her look-out
Walter Kinau, alias the writer
Gorch Fock.

S. M. S. Wiesbaden

HMS Defence.

Minnows v Leviathans:
The First Cruiser Squadron and the Wiesbaden

In the midst of the titanic clash of the battleships, two tragic and savage little dramas linked the fates of three British and one German cruiser. Local men were caught up in these actions and shared the agony of their German counterparts, many of whom had similar backgrounds and peacetime occupations

The British armoured cruisers in the Grand Fleet's 1st Cruiser Squadron were all sister ships of the same class and were highly praised by Naval publisher Jane's:
"These ships are singularly successful seaboats and are held by all who have served in them as the best cruisers ever turned out"

The Squadron was attached to Admiral Hood's battlecruiser squadron and entered the thick of the quickly escalating battle when Hood was sent to support Beatty's ships running North towards the Grand Fleet. Around 6pm Defence and Warrior broke away from HMS Duke of Edinburgh and Black Prince to finish off a crippled German cruiser that they spotted through the mist and smoke.

SMS Wiesbaden

A German light cruiser, the Wiesbaden was scouting ahead of the High Seas Fleet as the two battlefleets collided. Wiesbaden encountered the British battlecruisers and was quickly reduced to a flaming wreck. Her crew fought on until the end: it seems they made one last super human effort to launch a torpedo at the passing Grand Fleet as she sank, since it is likely that the torpedo which struck HMS Marlborough came from the Wiesbaden. The British cruisers Defence and Warrior spotted the burning ship and closed in to finish her off, only to fall victim to a similar fate.

HMS Black Prince.

HMS Warrior.

54

Wiesbaden was lost with all 889 hands, including Johann Kinau, better known by his pen name Gorch Fock. The son of a family of North Sea fishermen, he became famous in Germany for his stories about the sea and the coastal community he grew up in. He had transferred from the army to serve as a look-out on the Wiesbaden. The German navy subsequently named two sail training ships in his honour.

HMS Defence

Defence and Warrior's approach to the Wiesbaden quickly brought the two British ships into contact with the High Seas Fleet's Third Battle Squadron and Hipper's battlecruisers. The German big guns rained down heavy and accurate fire on both cruisers. HMS Defence's sudden, violent end at 6.20pm was witnessed from HMS Warspite:

"I saw three salvoes fall across her in quick succession, beauties. A flicker of flame ran aft along her forecastle head and up her fore funnel, which seemed to melt. Then whoof, up she went, a single huge sheet of flame, 500 feet high, mixed up with smoke and fragments. As it died down I saw her crumpled bow, red hot, at an angle of sixty degrees, and then she sank. I nearly vomited – God it was an awful sight – I couldn't get to sleep that night for thinking of it"
Captain Poland, Royal Marines, HMS Warspite

Tyneside papers published eyewitness stories from sailors after the battle:

"The Defence was hurled clean out of the water – Graphic account by survivors of HMS Warrior"

A number of local men were lost with the ship:
Francis Smith was born in 1891, one of 8 children, in Inverkeithing, Fife, but he was living in East Howdon and working as a railway porter by the 1911 Census. His wife Daisy Winifred was from Plymouth. He joined the Royal Navy when the war came and was an Acting Stoker on HMS Defence.

Thomas John Thomas was born in Bangor North Wales and was a student in the North East before the war. He was the Schoolmaster on HMS Defence. His brother Hugh Robert Thomas was also killed in the war.

Fred Cross was a turret operator before joining HMS Defence as a Leading Stoker. He was born in East Howdon in 1890 and married Katie Sarah Morrison in 1913. They had two children Hannah and James.

William Foster Gunn, was born in Milburn Place, North Shields in 1891, *"lost in action with HMS Defence, William F, beloved and only son of William F. and the late Margaret Gunn, 33 North Street, North Shields...deeply mourned by his loving father and sisters... he fought the good fight"*

HMS Warrior

Warrior barely survived her encounter with the German capital ships. Yet, as she was being pounded and hit by over 15 heavy shells, the battleship HMS Warspite passed by, her steering jammed, and the German heavy guns were turned on the capital ship. Captain Poland on board Warspite during this battering admitted to being sick with fear - and it can only have been worse for Warrior's crew,

"I was in the most dreadful sense of terror the whole time. Big gunfire is a beastly thing if you are the target. I don't want to go through anything like our bad quarter of an hour again"

Warspite's 'bad quarter of an hour' gave Warrior some respite and she was able to limp away from the fight. She was placed under tow by the seaplane carrier HMS Engadine but later had to be abandoned. Her crew was evacuated to Engadine, a desperate business given the sea conditions. As a result casualties on Warrior were comparatively light. Only one officer was killed and locally Artificer Frank Stevens of Newcastle was wounded.

HMS Black Prince

At 4.30pm Black Prince had played a small but significant role in the battle when she relayed the position of the German High Seas Fleet to Jellicoe by radio, after receiving a semaphore signal from HMS Lion which had lost her wireless mast. Later, when Defence and Warrior went after the Wiesbaden, Black Prince and Duke of Edinburgh remained with the Hood's battlecruiser squadron.

After the two battlefleets separated, Black Prince participated in the search to relocate the enemy. Around 1130pm Black Prince encountered the German battleline. Alone, and mistakenly assuming the German ships were friendly units in the darkness, she approached the enemy. Too late her crew realised the error and as she turned away, Black Prince was caught in a web of searchlight beams at a range of only 2000 yards. The cruiser soon met the same end as her two sisterships. The stronger German ships quickly smothered the British cruiser with over 20 heavy shells, and Black Prince was left to drift away and sink unseen with all 860 of her crew.

Local casualties amongst her crew included:

Able Seaman Alfred Charles Ansted of North Shields
Stoker J Rax of Newcastle
Able Seaman O Thorpe of Spennymoor.

Of the four ships of the 1st Cruiser Squadron, only Duke of Edinburgh returned from Jutland. The remaining ship of the class, HMS Achilles, was in the Tyne when battle- damaged ships arrived and had to be hurriedly undocked to make room for the fleet's casualties.

Jutland savagely demonstrated that old-style armoured cruisers simply could not survive in combat against the new generation of big gun warships.

The Buchanan brothers, Robert (left), Andrew (right).

HMS Fearless.

Two Newcastle Brothers at Jutland

Newcastle, Westgate, brothers Robert Blacklock Buchanan (born 1895) and Andrew Buchanan (born 1896) both saw action at Jutland on different ships.

Robert joined the 6th Tyne Division of the Royal Naval Volunteer Reserve in 1912 when he was 17. When war came he initially served in the cruiser HMS Devonshire, but by 11th April, 1916 he had passed the examination to become an Engine Room Artificer and he joined the light cruiser HMS Fearless on 26th April. The Fearless was at Jutland as the leader of the 1st Destroyer Flotilla, attached to Admiral Beatty's Battlecruiser Fleet, so Robert would have been involved in the action from its opening phases through to the conclusion at nightfall. One of the photo's from his family's collection is of the "Geordies of HMS Fearless", suggesting strong local affinities were maintained on board.

The younger brother, Andrew, joined the Royal Navy on 8th June, 1914 on a 12 year engagement. During the battle, Andrew was a gunner on the battlecruiser HMS Indomitable, part of Admiral Hood's 3rd Battlecruiser Squadron serving with the Grand Fleet. Along with Invincible and Inflexible, Andrew's ship was sent to reinforce Beatty's hard pressed ships as the two navies closed upon each other. He may have had the misfortune of witnessing HMS Invincible being ripped apart by the catastrophic explosion which sank her with most of her crew. A destroyer from his brother's flotilla rescued six survivors, but many more in the water were run down by passing ships, very possibly including the Indomitable.

Jutland took a psychological toll on Andrew, because he was discharged from a military hospital in September 1917 suffering from "neurasthenia", a contemporary term for "shell

The Geordies on HMS Fearless.

HMS Indomitable.

A few months before the great battle, The Times reported that the Royal Navy congratulated itself on having had fewer cases of neurasthenia than expected:

"In the Navy the anticipation of nervous disease has not been fully realized. Mental troubles of a really serious nature occurred in less than 1 per cent, and mild neurasthenic conditions in less than 4 per cent. Quite possibly this is due to the absence of alcoholism among the seamen, for, in the Fleet, the allowance of stimulant is only half a gill of rum daily, and special precautions are taken to prevent the men having more." 4th January, 1916

The Royal Navy's Surgeon General, H.D. Rolleston had just published a study, "The Influence of War on Disease", which optimistically thought improved health and physique from training and fresh air, the stamping out of venerial disease and control of alcohol consumption would stiffen the moral fibre of men to face the impact of new and deadly forms of war.

Andrew continued to suffer from mental health problems until he shot himself in 1923. His family blamed his wartime experiences for his suicide.

Robert Buchanan's granddaughter, Dot Tose, is a Northumbria World War One Project volunteer and kindly provided the photographs and biographical details reproduced here.

HMS Calliope.

HMS Calliope crew.

HMS Calliope At Jutland

Today's HMS Calliope is the Royal Navy's Reserve headquarters on the Tyne. In 1916 HMS Calliope was a light cruiser, and Commodore C E LeMesurier's flagship for the 4th Light Cruiser Squadron, operating in support of Admiral Hood's Battlecruiser force attached to the Grand Fleet. The ill-fated 1st Cruiser Squadron was also part of this section of the fleet.

When Hood was sent to support Beatty as the Grand Fleet and the High Seas Fleet approached each other, Calliope was soon involved in fierce fighting with German light cruisers, Hipper's battlecruiser squadron and some of the German battleships. It was during this phase of the battle that HMS Invincible was lost.

On board Calliope, Gunnery Petty Officer WJA Willis, was commanding a gun turret which was hit by a German shell: *"Wigg Bennett, my sight setter, was decapitated, his head falling in my lap. I was wounded in the left side. I can remember moving Wiggy Bennett's head, turning round to the crew and ordering the continuance of the action."*

Commodore LeMesurier wrote after the battle:
"My little act has been credited with two German destroyers and we claim a fat big battleship as well...Great pity the failing light and thick haze saved'em... we lost a lot of men, I'm afraid. Poor fellows, close on a dozen – and still a good many more crumpled up rather badly, wonderfully cheering over it all."

Although Calliope was not a Tyne-built ship, in the week after the battle the Newcastle Illustrated Chronicle published a picture of her crew, alongside positive reports of the Navy's battle in the North Sea.

The Adversaries

"Grosse Kreuzer, Gefechtswendung rein in den Feind! Ran!"
"Battlecruisers turn towards the enemy and engage him
closely! At him!"

The German Battlecruisers at Jutland

The German equivalents to ships like HMS Lion and HMS
Queen Mary were called "Grosse Kreuzer" or "Schlact Kreu-
zer"; there seems to have been some confusion in German
terminology, just as there was confusion in the Royal Navy's
battlecruiser doctrine. The Germans had five such ships at
Jutland (the weaker Blücher having been sunk the year before
at Dogger Bank and the Goeben gifted to Turkey):
Lützow (Hipper's flagship)
Moltke
Derfflinger
Von der Tann
Seydlitz
Named after famous generals from German history, they con-
stituted a single class and all were very similar.

Unlike their British equivalents, the German battlecruisers
were well protected by armour plate. Their 11" guns were
lighter than the 15" and 13.5" guns of the latest British battleships and battlecruisers, but as Jutland demonstrated, they
could be devastatingly effective. Compared with the over-
grown cruisers in Beatty's squadrons, the ships in Hipper's
force were in reality fast battleships.

The battlecruisers were the heroes of the German High Seas
Fleet at Jutland, involved in heavy fighting from the battle's
start mid-afternoon on 31st May until well into the early hours
of the following morning.

Damage to SMS Von der Tann.

SMS Moltke.

Outnumbered and outgunned at the outset of the fight with the British battlecruiser fleet, they quickly secured two devastating victories over the Indefatigable and Queen Mary. Taking up the pursuit during the Run to the North, they were the first German capital ships to be engaged by the dreadnoughts of the Grand Fleet. Despite a heavy pounding they were still able to inflict further catastrophic damage on HMS Invincible and several British cruisers.

When Admiral Scheer turned the German battleships away from the British and began his retreat, it was to his battlecruisers that he looked for a rear guard to delay the British pursuit. The German Navy's official history, 'Der Krieg in der Nordsee' (The War in the North Sea) described Jellicoe's battleships as, "an iron wall of 24 dreadnoughts". Twice Hipper's battered ships were ordered to turn towards this vastly more powerful enemy force and risk all to save the rest of their fleet.

Thrown repeatedly into the fighting, the five German battlecruisers suffered grievous damage. One of the Derfflinger's officer's recorded the impact of a heavy British shell on his ship:

"Several ships were engaging us at the same time...We were steaming at full speed into this inferno, offering a splendid target to the enemy while they were still hard to make out...Salvo after salvo fell around us, hit after hit struck our ship. At 8.13pm a serious catastrophe occurred, a 15 inch shell pierced the armour of 'Caesar' turret and exploded inside. The brave turret commander, Kapitanleutnant von Boltenstern, had both his legs torn off and with him nearly the whole gun crew were killed. The shell set on fire two charges in the turret, The flames from the burning charges spread to the transfer chamber, where they set fire to four more charges, and from these to the magazine, where four more were ignited. The burning cartridge cases emitted great tongues of flame which shot up out of the turrets as high as a house; but they only blazed, they did not explode as had been the case in the enemy battlecruisers. This saved the ship, but the result of the fire was catastrophe.

Damage to Derfflinger.

Seydlitz after the battle.

The huge tapering flames killed everyone within their reach. Of the seventy eight men inside the turret, only five managed to save themselves by climbing through the hole in the turret provided for throwing out empty shell cases, and of these several were seriously injured. The other seventy three men died together heroes in the fierce fever of battle loyally obeying the orders of their turret officer."

At 8.16pm she was hit again:

"A 15" shell pierced the roof of 'Dora' turret and here, too, exploded inside...the same horrors ensued. With the exception of a single man, who was thrown by the concussion through the turret entrance, the whole turret crew of eighty men, including all the magazine men, were killed instantly."

The Lützow eventually succumbed to the damage inflicted by 24 hits from heavy shells, and had to be abandoned. To prevent the floating wreck being captured the ship was sunk by German torpedoes. Some of her crew were still trapped alive below deck when the ship was scuttled.

At the end of the battle, the remaining ships were in a bad state. Derfflinger and von der Tann reported that each had only two guns still operational. Derfflinger had a large hole ripped in her side that was open to the sea. Fires started by British shells had turned parts of her interior into a "volcano". Shattered compartments were filled with debris and human body parts.

The Seydlitz was barely afloat and was incapable of putting up a fight. Only expert seamanship brought her home. During the last stages of the voyage her flooded hull was scraping over sandbanks. She had to be temporarily beached when she reached the coast to be pumped out before risking taking her through the channel into the harbour, which she could easily have blocked if she sank. She had taken on 5,000 tons of water and had been hit more than 30 times during the battle.

Repaired in the months following the battle, the surviving German battlecruisers were amongst the core of the High Seas Fleet that the victorious allies insisted were to be interned at Scapa Flow in 1919. On arrival they sailed past Admiral Beatty, who had previously claimed he had sunk several of them.

Battle damage to Derfflinger.

Jutland – Blame And Scandal

"I know we were fearfully surprised when we came in to hear that all the people thought it was disgraceful, but I don't think anybody minded as we were all rather pleased with ourselves. The Daily Mail says it is a drawn battle so I suppose it's a pretty complete victory for us." Commander TS Fox Pitt, June 1916

Although the population of Tyneside greeted the returning ship's companies as heroes and the Navy thought it had achieved a victory, the country was soon disenchanted when it heard of the disparity in losses between the Royal Navy and the Germans. In part, the situation may have arisen from the rather terse press notice issued by the Admiralty, which did not announce the 'second Trafalgar' the public had been led to expect.

The loss of the battlecruisers came as a shock given the way the ships had been lauded before the war. Investigations at the time blamed their loss on inadequate armour, although one modern writer has also pointed out the poor quality of the ammunition used, which both failed to damage the enemy and proved unstable when stored, plus the lack of adequate internal blast protection around the magazines. Recent research has also indicated that Beatty's force may have deliberately overridden safety procedures by leaving blast doors open to increase the speed of reloading.

As the scale of the losses became clear, and that the Germans had apparently been allowed to escape, the press and the public soon looked for a scapegoat. This proved to be Admiral Jellicoe, whose caution was unfavourably compared with Beatty's desire to chase after the enemy. Jellicoe's career soon came to an end and he retired from the Navy.

His reputation was unfairly tarnished at the time and into the post war period, firstly by Winston Churchill's comments in

The German fleet at Scapa Flow, 28 November 1918.

After scuttling the Derfflinger is towed away on a floating dry dock in the 1930's.

his history of the war; *The World Crisis* (when First Lord of the Admiralty, he had promoted Beatty despite the objections of the Navy), and secondly by Filson Young's articles in the Daily Express, who wrote:

"...in the midst of a battle, there is not always time to observe the rules of the parade ground. Opportunity was there, but did not wait long enough for Admiral Jellicoe"

Within the Navy, many senior officers were far more inclined to support the admiral. There was outrage in some quarters when it was learned that an official report on the battle was suppressed by Beatty upon his promotion to First Sea Lord, because it highlighted the, "signal inefficiency of the battle cruiser fleet". The most outspoken defence of Jellicoe came from Admiral Sir Reginald Bacon, who wrote several letters to the papers and eventually published *The Jutland Scandal* to set out his case that criticsm of Jellicoe and praise of Beatty was an:

"indulgence in glorious action rather than the cold business of war".

Conclusions

So was this battle a draw, a German or a British victory?

The casualty lists and ships lost do suggest an outcome in the Germans' favour, however these 'scores' are deceptive. No one can doubt the skill and courage of the sailors in the young Imperial German Navy, and their ships were undoubtedly more robust than some of their British counterparts.

A significant proportion of British losses were due to the design flaws of the battlecruisers. An innovative concept, originally they had not been intended to go anywhere near a battle such as Jutland. Although they represented catastrophic losses in terms of lives and damage to public opinion, they did not fundamentally impact on the balance of power between the two fleets. The other Royal Navy losses at Jutland were of a comparable order to the German's.

The German object was to break British naval supremacy and the blockade of their ports – this they failed to do. Despite the losses the Royal Navy remained stronger than the German fleet after the battle, and the damage German ships suffered at Jutland probably increased Britain's advantage. In the face of these facts, their true position slowly dawned on the Germans: they had been given one opportunity at grasping a victory and it had been lost.

"our fleet losses were, despite the luck that smiled on us, severe, and in June 1916 it was clear to every knowledgeable person that this battle must be, and would be, the only one."
Berliner Tageblatt 1918

Aftermath

The High Seas Fleet did make further forays into the North Sea after Jutland, but it never met the British Grand Fleet again until after the end of hostilities. It was increasingly clear that U-boats not battleships offered the German Navy the best means of defeating Britain. In 1917 the Germans adopted a policy of unrestricted submarine warfare. At one point it seemed as if this would force Britain to sue for peace or face starvation, but the Royal Navy was able to turn the tide by adopting the convoy system and new technology. For the Germans their U-boat policy was a diplomatic disaster as their attacks on neutral ships hastened the United States into the war on the allied side.

In 1918 the German High Seas Fleet finally entered Scapa Flow, not as victors but as prisoners of war. 370 allied ships – British, French and American - greeted the nine best remaining German battleships, seven light cruisers and forty nine torpedo boats off the coast of Scotland. One of the German officers commented,

"...the deployment of such overwhelming strength looked like a grudging recognition of the former power of the High Seas Fleet."

Unable to accept this humiliation, the German crews eventually scuttled their ships and sent them to the seabed. Great ships like the Derfflinger ended up as ignominious scrap metal.

The German fleet begin scuttling at Scapa Flow, May 1919.

The Fate of the Dreadnoughts

The great dreadnought fleets of World War One soon proved to be useless to both defeated and victor alike and a great many of the Jutland capital ships were scrapped during the 1920s.

The Royal Navy would continue to build new battleships in the '20s and '30s, and deploy them throughout the Second World War. Britain's last super dreadnought, HMS Vanguard, was launched in 1946, but it was evident before 1939 that their nemesis had arrived twofold - in the submarine and the aircraft carrier.

Survivor

The only surviving ship that fought at Jutland is the light cruiser HMS Caroline, undergoing renovation in Belfast and due to open to the public in the summer of 2016.

HMS Caroline in 2015.

APPENDIX 1

A Provisional List of Local Casualties at Jutland

Alphabetically by ship, showing each man's name and home town or Royal Naval Volunteer Reserve division. Where the spelling of a name is unclear in newspaper reports this is indicated.

HMS Black Prince

Ansted, Alfred Charles, Tynemouth
Babbins, John, Tyne Division RNVR
Binns, Ernest, Tyne Division RNVR
Braime, George Herbert, Tyne Division RNVR
Dixon, Robert M, Cambois
Hickson, Arthur, Tyne Division RNVR
Kimber, Joseph, Swalwell
Lamb, JA, Gateshead
McBride, Cyril, Tyne Division RNVR
Parter, John, Tyne Division RNVR
Pegford, Ernest Lynn, Tyne Division RNVR
Rax, J, Newcastle
Taylor, FG, Byker
Thomas, Hilton, Tyne Division RNVR
Turnbull, James, Tyne Division RNVR
Wood, JW, Blyth

HMS Defence

Bartrum, Thomas, Heaton
Brookes, Philip Howard, Tyne Division RNVR
Cowen, John James, Tyne Division RNVR
Cross, Frederick, East Howden
Gibson, John, Whitley Bay
Gunn, William Foster, Jarrow
Henderson, Robert Stanley, Tyne Division RNVR
Jowle, Walter, Tyne Division RNVR
Nunn, Charles Arthur, Tyne Division RNVR
Pearson, John, Tyne Division RNVR
Sandlands/Sandilands?, John, Jarrow
Smith, Francis, Tynemouth
Thomas, Thomas John, Tynemouth
Wise, James William, South Shields

HMS Indefatigable

Bennett, John, Tynemouth
Builth, W W, South Shields
Cowell, W E, Heaton
Freestone, Charles Allan, Tyne Division RNVR
Green, Randall, Tyne Division RNVR
Hedley, George, Bebside
Houghland, Ernest, Tynemouth
Johnson, J, Byker
Larkman, Alfred, Newcastle
Lock, Henry, South Shields
Lock, Richard, Tyne Division RNVR
Michaux, James, Tynemouth
Robson, Matthew, Newcastle
Robson, Henry M, Newcastle
Sheard, Arthur, Tyne Division RNVR
Smith, William Waugh, South Shields
Thomson, William, Tynemouth
Urquhart, Arthur S, Benwell
Weatherstone, Robert Hunter, North Shields
White, Richard, Willington Quay

HMS Invincible

Bank, Thomas, Choppington
Briggs, John, Blyth
Budge?, W, Wallsend
Calder, A, Benwell
Callender, Peter, South Shields
Davey, William, Newcastle
Elkin?, Thomas, Tyne Division RNVR
Fahley, A, Newcastle
Fox, Thomas, Newcastle (Royal Marines)
Hands, Charles Clark, Tyne Division RNVR
Hold, Albert, Tynemouth
Holliday, J B, Blyth
Hunter, William, Tyne Division RNVR
McCulloch, John, Wallsend
Mitchell, George William, Gateshead
Parkin, Septimus?, Felling
Pentland, William George, Newcastle
Shaw, Henry, Tyne Dock
Southall, Archibald Henderson, Shiremoor
Taylor, Joseph, Hexham

HMS Lion

Dinning, George, Jarrow
Fagan, Patrick, Jarrow

HMS Marlborough
Monk, George Edgar, Tynemouth (Burial)

HMS New Zealand
McLaughlin, Joseph, Jarrow
Gillan, John, Jarrow

HMS Queen Mary
Aitken, Thomas, Tyne Dock
Anderson, S, Newcastle
Atkinson, William, Tynemouth
Barnett, Joseph, Newcastle
Brighouse, James Henry, South Shields
Buckham, George, South Shields
Campion, James, Tynemouth
Cowper, P G, Byker
Currie/Curry?, Richard, Gateshead
Dale, J, Newcastle
Dodd, George, West Moor
Dryburgh, Robert, Tynemouth
Ford, Robert, Gateshead
Glais/Glads?, J S, Gateshead
Graham, James Francis, North Shields
Graves, Robert, Jarrow
Hull, John, Gateshead
Kelly, James, Tynemouth
Kewney, George Stanley, Tynemouth
Lisle, Alexander, Newcastle
Litster, Alexander, Tynemouth
McKeoman, Hugh, Jarrow
Percival, R R, Newcastle
Rickaby, Stephen, Newcastle
Roe, Richard Henry, Whitley Bay
Roe or Rowe?, R H, Willington Quay
Simpson, W, Benwell
Sparrow, J, Benwell
Stephenson, Thomas Edward, Seaton Burn
Stewart, Robert, Wallsend
Sweet, J, Ashington
Swinney, James Robson, West Moor
Tait, Edward, Tynemouth
Tempest, Edward A, Newcastle
Tuck, Joseph, Gateshead
Waugh, Charles, Forest Hall
Weatherby, W, Blyth
White, Frederick Ernest, North Shields
Wilkinson, George, Heaton,

HMS Tipperary

English, John, Wallsend
Jackson, W, Ashington
Wear, T A, Newcastle

HMS Turbulent

Sullivan, John, Elswick
Tittley, A S, Newcastle

HMS Warrior

Mason, Isaac, Dudley
Stevens, Frank, Newcastle

Vessel Unknown

Bax, Arthur, Newcastle
Gray, John, Newcastle
Hardy, W, Walbottle
Harrison, Thomas, Newcastle
Healy, Richard, Blyth
Young, J H, Low Fell

APPENDIX 11

HMS Calliope Casualties at Jutland

From information provided by Lt Cdr Duncan Young, HMS Calliope

Killed

Joseph Skidmore, Stoker 1st Class
Thomas Edward Sutcliffe, Stoker Royal Naval Reserve
William Frank Rowlingson, Able Bodied Seaman
Thomas Joseph Hogan, Officer's Steward
Walter William Fairweather, Able Bodied Seaman
Archer William Balcombe, Sergeant Royal Marine Light Infantry
Frederick Thomas Horsfall, Private Royal Marine Light Infantry
Henry C Bennett, Able Bodied Seaman (aka "Wiggy" - Sight Setter on a 4" gun)

Died of Wounds

William Alfred Collins, Private Royal Marine Light Infantry
Thomas Joseph Trish, Able Bodied Seaman
Sidney Thomas Ellis, Able Seaman

Severely Wounded

Bertram Raleigh Bickford, Staff Surgeon Royal Navy

Seriously Wounded

James H Hines, Able Bodied Seaman
William R Walker, Boy 1st Class
James Halcrow, Leading Signaller
Herbert J Bowtell, Able Seaman
James Orton, Stoker Royal Naval Reserve

Wounded

Matthew McClure, Mate Royal Navy
Frederick William Moody, Stoker 1st Class
James Hickman, Engineering Artificer
William A Bird, Ordnance Seaman
Charles Purchase, Sick Berth Staff
William J A Willis, Petty Officer (commanded a 4"gun)
John Zammatt, Officer's Cook 1st Class
Malcolm J Cooper, Leading Seaman
William G Bethell, Leading Seaman
Charles Evans, Leading Seaman
Percy Hutton, Ordnance Seaman
Harry Simpkins, Boy 1st Class
Stanley Wright, Boy 1st Class
Robert Fryett, Able Seaman
William Fraser, Plumber
George H J Huxtable, Private Royal Marine Light Infantry
George W Willison, Private Royal Marine Light Infantry

Printed in Great Britain
by Amazon